Made in India

Jen Gibson

Made in India

travels in poetry

Made in India: travels in poetry
ISBN 978 1 74027 986 4
Copyright © text Jen Gibson 2015

First published 2015 by
Ginninderra Press
PO Box 3461 Port Adelaide SA 5015
www.ginninderrapress.com.au

Contents

Shivaliks	7
Shiv's Falcon	8
Crocus	9
George	10
Kingfisher	11
Smiling Teeth	12
Exile after Exile...	13
Loose Motions	14
Chuha	15
Krishna at the YWCA	16
Lord of Udaipur	17
Walnuts from Kashmir	18
'Mr Gurdip is out of station'	19
Friends now,	20
Monsoon Moments	21
A Blessing?	22
Ahimsa	23
Surprise	24
Cottonwool Sky	25
Venerable Rishi	26
Next Time	27
Choices	28
Uninvited	29
Tibetan	30
Soirée	31
Like mangoes	32
First Impressions	33
Mahakala	34
Forgetting	35
Hair	36

Buddha	37
Squirrel Charm	38
In Memorial	39
Old Delhi	40
but a dream…	41
Starting out	42
Happy Valley	43
Amber Fort, Jaipur	44
Train to Kerala	45
Rajasthani Craftsman	47
Till	48
Pink Swish	49
Like Pharaohs	50
In Agra	51
Pre Exam	52
Palace–Hotel	53
Behind the Poems	54

Shivaliks

jagged peaks that dip and rise
        a far-stretching line
                of white meringue

if I could use my tongue
        lick soft-serve ice cream
                on a giant's scale
I'd have formed you

vast Indian serpent range
        cloud flecked
                beneath me.

Shiv's Falcon

Surely Shiv
       if I ingest your *bhang*
            your opium

                 I will fly too

      leap from my window
           on this green, exultant morn

soar serene over mountain heavens
      loop and circle
           buoyant on air-sea

                scan creation

know your bliss of being.

Crocus

Suddenly you come
        bursting pink delight
        by rock and mountain

under trees filled
        with discarded plastic bags

delicate sun-drawn crocus.

George

George,
> 'Father George'

your name's gloomy as
> my ancient uncle

but you, most definitely, aren't.

Dark and vibrant
> your bearded face sparkles
> open, flirting, innocence

your beaming white smile
> jolts my heart

and that sharp Jesuit twist of mind
> nudges my thoughts in fresh directions

If only you were not
> 'untouchable'…

Kingfisher

surveying your kingdom from
        electric wires
                folded wings unruffled

rich splashes of colour
                that hint at more

till I see in flight

        your outspread wings of
                startling blue.

Smiling Teeth

                There's one on top
        another beneath
                              two at the rear

What more is needed
        for a good chomp
        in old age

for that smile
        of a young bride
                beaming her love
                        for Lord Krishna.

Exile after Exile...

I sit down –
(an Australian taking refuge from Western ways)
slurp *thugpa* with noodles

in the warm cafeteria
a soulful African-America voice
recalls the ancient Jewish Diaspora of Babylon

this Tibetan exile
has lasted generations,
children learn three alien tongues to thrive

diminutive *Dawa* cradles
one last cup of chai

another journey

soon she'll be gone, in the damp taxi
wending from Delhi to Boston

blessed with flowing white *Katag** draped about her shoulders.

* *Katag*: a Tibetan ceremonial scarf

Loose Motions

Catch phrase from a bygone era
    'Just say you have "Loose motions"!'

'Please, Miss,' asks the small girl, 'What is "loose motions"?'

She sits on my mat, playing Patience
    making excruciating smells.

What are loose motions?
    Jai India's answer to the
common cold.

Chuha

The moon, near-full,
shines brightly through my window
casting magic shadows across mountains

there's rustling again

could there be   another rat.

Oh Ratty,
      where is my anger, hatred
                              my indignation
…now I can't hear your gnawing
      so disturbing   sleep destroying

I lie and wonder
            are you
                                dead inside my trap.

Waking, I see you've eaten
      peanuts, potato chips, bananas

the trap remains
      untriggered.

Why am I so glad
      when you've made
            such a smelly, awful, untouchable mess

and outsmarted me again.

Krishna at the YWCA

The young women have grown old
>very old
in this dilapidated Christian mausoleum
>of monsoon damp
>female misery
this shrine to long gone values
>from another clime
>>another time.

Seated beneath Christ crucified
>you, charming, military Krishna
>administer a bygone era
>continue your age-old playful, trickster
>gallant with female, wiles.

Where is the Shepherd King now?
>Am I a *Radha* among these adoring milk-maidens
>enchanted by your flute?

The Shepherd King has gone
>back to the green and pleasant land
the maidens all passed their prime.

Here beside faded Christian slogans
you've placed your deities.

There's   Ganesha with his elephant head.
Here's   Lakshmi sparkling bling and wealth.

Beneath Christ crucified
>Shiva with his trident
>>strides boldly forward.

You go too far, Lord Krishna.

Lord of Udaipur

Proud Rajasthani Warrior,
> unconquered Lord, enthroned in your
>> auto-rickshaw chariot

by fountain greenery and gentle breezes
> you enfold my ears
> cup one smooth hand each side
> till I can hear an echo of monsoon sounds

you pin a white flower to my hair
> pluck a stemless, pink, rosebud
> for my hand
> whisper promises of love.

The summer palace glistens on its lake

> washer-people pound clothes with sticks
>> lay them to dry
>> wave off stray cows

> pilgrims tread ancient water steps.

With our last touching of hands
> the promised closeness of bodies
> remains unfulfilled

Across the water
> inviting yet unexplored, the White Palace.

Walnuts from Kashmir

There's no greater hook
        than this magic name

                      Kashmir

for one who longs to see
       snow-capped mountains
             lotus-filled lakes
                   vales of flowering saffron…

Though twice the cost of others
       I must have these nuts

And they're all I hope
       and more
             much more

two hemispheres of
       crisp, fresh, biting succulence

insatiable I devour walnuts
       wondering if
             I'll ever roam
                   their troubled birthplace.

'Mr Gurdip is out of station'

Wearing technology
as the British their tropical hats,
he plies outlying regions
seeking profit.

We underlings remain on duty for
        a sale, repair or print out…

if it's simple we might handle it

but when Mr Gurdip is   out of station
don't hope for scanning,
successful fax transmission
or viral checks

for these you have to wait
till the Sahib returns   from   his tour of duty.

Friends now,

you no longer
bother to move
as I take my towel
or dip into food-filled
plastic bags
on our shared table.

Your elegant
eight-legged shape
unmoving
accepts the inevitability
of my being here.

Monsoon Moments

Morning mist descends on
disembodied snatches
of childish conversation and
girlish laughter far below

as mist thickens
the sounds of a flute
waft sweet and thin
over the valley

poignant fragile notes

A Blessing?

Rain, rain, rain
heavy, misty rain

though we walk under umbrella hats
the dampness creeps

torrents gush down slopes
make rivers

startled tourist shelter
beside resigned locals.

You depart today   maybe forever
following your   dream of freedom

by Tibetan reckoning
this rain's   a blessed omen

May it be so.

Ahimsa

Elusive butterfly
I long to reach out, enfold you
in my cupped hand

unlock the enigma of your
fragile mystery.

Reluctant, I watch you fly away…

Surprise

A landslide of unexpected joy

dahlias among green
        growing in topsy-turvy profusion

                vivid yellows
                        deep glorious reds
                              pinks and
                                          startling orange

floating, beyond the autumn equinox
in mountain sunlight.

Cottonwool Sky

White balls of fairy-floss that
hang in dense grey skies
above the peaks
send out
exploratory tendrils
elongated, ghostly fingers
that probe
into valleys where
feeble lights of human habitation
flicker to fade
as the sun's greater 'neon light'
begins
to spread
radiance anew.

Venerable Rishi

We row on Mother Ganga
trail wistful fingers in water
between flowers and lantern
coracles, fashioned from
banana fronds

I bask in the warmth of your spiritual
ecology
        philosophies of purity
                and heavenly renewal

Charred corpses pass
                disassembled remnants

So many objects to be accepted
                in the sacred stream
                        by the River Goddess.

Next Time

As I come down those few familiar
steps, turn and cross my balcony

                                  I see him

Tough as a nuggety boxer
the male monkey

                                  retreats to my bed

why did I leave that door ajar

                                  he's startled too

beady round eyes stare belligerent
gauge my fear

one pink palm   so like my own
snatches the jar of sweets
beside my bed

chewing off the lid
with long incisors
he stares defiance

Can he know these eucalypts
hold a precious link   to my homeland.

My startled cries bring help
experienced humans   drive the intruder out

I fling the bitten plastic jar
      its tragic contents

                                  into the rubbish.

Choices

India's like
two smart men

one targets
much, much money
success – the delights of gold
        palatial abodes
                costly goods
he chases Kama – the sexiness of
life, lived to its full
        at any cost

The other opts-out of worldly ways
        tries non-attachment
        prefers unpaved roads
        and homelessness

thinking it brings
true freedom.

Uninvited

So many intruders

huge spiders pace the walls

rag-winged moths arrive
with night, in the company
of mosquitoes and midges

portly, bottle-nosed rats flee
flooded burrows
jump sightless between furniture
spill oil and rice
squawk anxiety, gnaw plastic lids

swerving in chaos on thin feet
their tails sweep
provisions everywhere
till their trauma is mine.

Tibetan

exiles
poor women
in shabby dresses
who work with tired
tireless hands
gnarled fingers, bent knees
stooped backs

work into old age
cracking rocks with
picks, a
base for these
alarming mountain roads

women who work
endlessly with
grey devoted faces.

Soirée

Shades (a fashion statement
of corporate India)
mask friendly eyes, as
your genial bulk waits my approach

garlanded with wide and gracious smiles
(descendant of Moguls)
your open hands
extend an invitation
(conquest through charm)

It's a grand invitation to
a kingly Durbar
endowed by your liege lord

Nestlé International.

Like mangoes

A large black hump swells on his strong
brown back as
the bull plods, ponderous
and slow

unperturbed
by rain, his
balls hang like
swinging mangoes.

First Impressions

Dry, flat, Rajasthan, where
camels pull wooden-wheeled carts
between vivid women
                 veils, skirts, chemise a
                      splendid cacophony of colour

round pyramid stacks of hay
        stand beside mud and straw
            finger-patted homes and

red-slate, matchbox shapes
        wait to be puffed over
            by the big bad wolf
                 in his white turban.

Mahakala

Above Bodh Gaya's ancient
charnel grounds
where birds of coarse
disposition
flock and shrill,
there lies an ancient cave

a powerful place
(known long to humans)
whose death-dark interior
offers a strange peace,
the bliss of fear-free Being

a sense of those who once,
having loosed the bonds
of time
have
no other burden.

Forgetting

Why do I think pensively
of writing to relatives
no longer in this
'living' world

Separate in 'space'
by continents from
beloved ones
I confuse
'time' as well.

Hair

You will not cut your hair   ever
it's piled in a high topknot
covered with cloth.

He must forever shave his
monthly, on full-moon day.

Symbols of difference   and belonging.

Buddha

India's greatest export
marketable for
millennia

after various
suitable modifications
to the original product.

Squirrel Charm

Endearing squirrel
you retrieve crumbs from my bread with
sharp and quirky movements,
retreat with a swirl of
your elegant tail

the inquisitive twitch of your
curious nose speaks of our shared
delight in exploration

my mind makes you a friend

                                    never foe

though in truth
you differ so little from

                        a rat.

In Memorial

Ferns on the trunks of trees
turn brown and dry as
monsoon departs

delicate sepals of white and
green and gold
open their vulnerable centres to
a fragile sun

veined nasturtium leaves
support spider webs,
ethereal constructions
woven in gossamer, that
quiver with a footfall.

Those women quiver too
at the sudden, violent
assault

police guns open fire

in that instant serenity shatters

screams of injured females
(marchers for justice)
pierce the
foggy beauty
in a lethal childbirth

our new 'hilly' state
Uttarakhand
is born –
torn from the wombs of
fallen mothers.

Old Delhi

Dressed all in white
you evoke Divine Creation
the Dance of Life, its
endless enchantment
weaving cruel delights.

Above this private court of begums
on high walls, seeking cool reprieve
we watch
long-tailed, square kites
high-flung over the crowded city
they too seek freedom from the
giant ogress below.

You recreate the greatness of Mogul ancestors
their living architecture
       – so here and now right-functioning
(four walls hiding a family paradise within)

explain how Barbar once loved a young boy
(himself perhaps)
loved fleetingly and lost, on his
journey of invasion over the Khyber
(he then choosing women and conquest).

You utter the unspeakable sadness of
Partition – Nehru, Jinnah, Mountbatten –
       of those trapped wrong side of the line.

Hot day turns to night and
the moon (once so full)
wanes in the cooling sky.

but a dream...

Once I knew a nursery rhyme

> *Row, row, row, your boat*
> *Gently down the stream*

Now it's mechanical melody
issues from the part-built construction site
(devoid of fence or garden) –
a wealthy Delhi home in making

> *Merrily, merrily, merrily, merrily*

a newly fitted America device
for water purification
chirps, into the morning

> *Merrily, merrily, merrily, merrily*
> *life is but a dream.*

a very strange dream.

Starting out

Soon noise and dust and heat
will chase the cool, damp, lingering morn
from the open windows of this train

Sounds of motor scooters
                    'India's limousines'
will begin again, as I speed on
in one of 'India's helicopters'
                    this long-distance train.

Happy Valley

Birds chirp spring from
lapis-bright skies

far above there's snow on
the mountain peaks

lofty green deodars
(scented Himalayan cedars)
tall and spreading
drop their load of
wintery snow
stride down
to the school

charmed, they listen, beside
geranium, marigold and cornflower
(gay plants in pots)
to the sweet call of
young school voices
chanting lessons in unison.

Amber Fort, Jaipur

From the walled citadel
elephants bathing below
make moving miniatures
three happy trunks, playing tricks
spraying water –
trumpeting, wading, submerging
unaware.

This mountain fastness
cooled by soft breezes over water
its courtyards a pleasance of flowers
where scents of jasmine and
with evening
radhki rani
flow indoors to
the Maharaja's chamber
towering above the rest

there, in the darkness
four candles illumine the whole,
curved walls of coloured gems and mirror
sparkle tiny balls of faceted light
onto the ceiling dome
create an evening universe of
twinkling jewels, a paradise
where lovers must embrace.

Train to Kerala

I

A buffalo grazes in a passing
field, beside the rail-line
linking there to here.
Two small birds hitch
a ride on the back of their
huge bovine transporter and
speculate on the pickings
continual munching may
disturb for them.
On a sudden whim, one of them
darts away, takes a new
flight path

II

beside me on the sleeper train
a sweet Christian nun
veiled in white, splutters
and sniffs, fighting the flu and
continual travel from far north
to dark south (where her
Mother House lies). She
sneezes like a hooter
coughs away the distance
between her vocation
and her family

III

outside a rhinoceros
sinks its great bulk into
water, pleasurably submerges
to its horn.
One crow paddles its back while
another perches proprietorial on
the flat surface
between the ears
of its vast host.

Rajasthani Craftsman

The white turban's wound proud with
metre on metre of fine cotton cloth
wound firm above the aged beauty
of your fine-chiselled face
above this thick black moustache
so prized by your people.

You stretch, align and twang
blue-powdered string
till it forms construction lines
straight and true
on the green grass

through aeons
the gnarled and knotted sinews
of your arms and calves
(strong and sound as an old oak)
were formed through work

not satisfied with skills of lesser men
you climb aloft yourself on
swaying bamboo scaffolding
in hot sun,
apply dollops of cement
smoothed with the precision of a baker
the trowel caress of a lover

and what a lover you must have been
regal, confident and devoted
in the service of your Raja.

Till

You remove your gleaming gold ring
pass it to your wife who
fits it to her smaller, middle finger

your whole family watches, anxious –
mother, father, sisters, children
no one speaks.

The ring will stay with your wife
waiting your safe return
from the greedy city.

Pink Swish

Barefoot women are sweeping
swish, swish, swish
their hand-held brooms
connect with stone and dirt

already it's warm and birds sing
fully awake, sing, as
children begin to chant their Hindi alphabet

so many little birds, busy in the
early morning.

The Pink City, fortress of Rajputs
grows through desert sands by
barren hills

its scalloped arches lead
to watered gardens where
trees mute the fierce sunlight to dapple,
host the buzz of insects

reviving scents of jasmine, frangipani,
hibiscus, waft on green air and

tomorrow, the swish of gentle brooms
below these same pink arches
will clear the fallen leaves again
as birds call and children chant.

Swish, swish, swish.

Like Pharaohs

'Hilly' women out on the slopes
wield small curved scythes
harvest fresh monsoon grasses

wearing scarves like pharaohs their
long plaits linked behind
they call one another
(happy voices on the clear mountain air)

step by step the cliff's laid bare
village legs – sturdy and sinuous
support the bend and thrust of working bodies
earrings and bright beads jingle
on sleeveless jackets

plaited to strands, long grass
binds smaller bundles into one large whole
trussed with thin hemp rope

the huge bundles (small bushes too)
rest, with the help of friends,
on heads and backs

hands swing free
steady the bulky loads
for the steep return

Fortunate cows –
more privileged than children –
soon to enjoy
banquets of devoted greenery.

In Agra

The evening Taj glows
luminous against the
vault of wind-smeared sky, white
on fading blue

whiter still this igloo-dome
late flower of Mogul summers
resting beside Yamuna's failing flow

on the further shore
cattle graze and
past flows to present.

She (Mumtaz Mahal) was
(Shah Jahan's) third wife, he
lost her to their fourteenth child
a daughter, sweeter by far to
his youngest son

      Aurangzeb
(that near patricide)
imprisoned his pater in the Red Fort
      left him to die

there, through fluted arches
a deposed father views
his perfect lotus with its peak
of gold

will its marbled symmetry
(beauty created from loss)
sustain the ageing Shah in his
final trial.

Pre Exam

Fresh from morning ablutions
hair severely combed, you arrive
to wait composed, till
my bucket bath's complete

side by side
        we discuss those fearful
        study notes
obscure outdated things
        where Dickens
                (a young man still) is alive and well

archaic nonsense from
        long-gone times in
                another place
that you must swat, for this exam.

I wish you many blessings
as you trudge to your doom.

Palace–Hotel

The Rajput's noble crest
hangs on ancient entrance gates
        cast in Glasgow of finest British steel
        strong to endure
        more centuries

Crafted in pure gold:

        the smiling Hindu Sun
        his dazzling moustache and
        Hanuman (the Monkey King)
        bearing aloft (in one hand)
        the gift of
        a huge, peaked mountain
        laden with healing herbs.

Two hundred years on and
the chandelier from Prague
still hangs in the carved hall
by magnificent portraits,
memorials to turbaned
Rajput warriors in dazzling robes, adorned
with pearls, their
sword hilts glowing rubies.

Today, paying guests maintain
these records of grandeur, suspended
        beside those English monarchs
        Edward, George, Victoria,
        beside the dead Lord Curzon.

Behind the Poems

The experiences that inspired these poems took place in the 1990s when I lived in India (with various breaks outside the country) for a period of four years. No doubt India has changed a lot since then – I know I have. At that time I was researching the life of Ashoka, an exceptional leader who lived around 250 BCE. I travelled extensively, read and wrote copiously in mountain retreats, and taught English (from time to time).

Visiting a wide range of regions, I experienced some of the extraordinary diversity in ethnicity, geography, history and food that is India. I stayed with Christian nuns and Tibetan Buddhist monks. For the longest periods, I resided in the mountains, firstly around Mussoorie (then in Uttar Pradesh,* above Dehra Dun) and later in a small village, approachable only by a mountain track outside Manali, Kulu Valley, Himachal Pradesh. I travelled widely, mostly by train but also by bus and car.

Because I love the Himalayas, there are probably more poems from these mountain experiences, yet Kerala and the south (in fact everywhere), are so full of wonder, filth, beauty, kindness and vitality. Exasperation transforms to joy in the merest instant and I always felt fully alive living in India.

As a featured poet at Poets Republic coordinated by Liz Wingfield at the Republic Bar, North Hobart, and sponsored by the Tasmanian Writers Centre, I read a selection of poems from India in 2012. Jan Colville's enthusiasm encouraged me to do something with them. Ron Pretty was kind enough to read and provide valuable feedback and Robyn Mathison has carefully read and commented on most of these poems in preparation. Poetry workshops with Gina Mercer and earlier with the wonderful,

---

* See the poem 'In Memorial'.

irrepressible Judith Rodriguez in Melbourne, and occasional poetic dialogues with Esther Ottaway (when we both worked at the Tasmanian Writers Centre) were all sources of inspiration. Some poems were workshopped at Diggers, a poetry group I belonged to for several years in Hobart. Its members included Karen Armstrong, Susan Austin, Jenny Barnard, Jan Colville, Mike Cooper, Steve Isham, Lorraine Haig and Anne Scott. Nancy Schaffner has willingly read my work and offered warm, supportive feedback. The Fellowship of Australian Writers, Tasmania members provided some feedback at their monthly meetings, while Mary Jenkins, Megan Schaffner, Anne Kellas, Kathryn Lomer and other poet friends offered encouragement.

It is with great respect for all the support offered to me and so many Australian writers, that I thank Stephen Matthews and Brenda Eldridge of Ginninderra Press for making the publication of *Made in India: travels in poetry* possible.

Dear Reader, I hope that you can visualise and enjoy at least some of these journeys through India in poetry. Because they were precious for me, I attempt to share them here. Please forgive any cultural (or creature) insensitivities you feel may have crept in.

May all things Made in India continue to thrive.

Jen Gibson
Cygnet, Tasmania, 2015

www.ingramcontent.com/pod-product-compliance
Lightning Source LLC
Chambersburg PA
CBHW062204100526
44589CB00014B/1944